Food Truck
Owner's Handbook

The Entrepreneur's Guide to Street Food Success

By Andrew Moorehouse

A Free Gift for You

As a thank you for your purchase, I'm making my book **Food Truck Vehicles and Equipment** available to you for free.

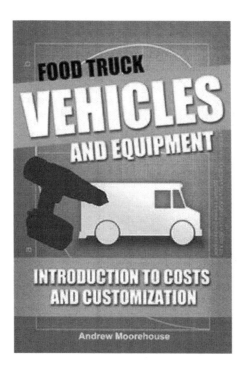

You'll get an introduction to food trucks and the vehicles used in the industry. In this booklet, you can find some basic costs of buying a food truck and learn about what food truck builders can do for you.

Visit the URL below for this exclusive offer:

TheFoodTruckStartup.com/free

Table of Contents

Introduction

Starting your own business is not an easy task! It doesn't matter if it is a large or small business; there will always be roadblocks and challenges you will face along the way. Brick and mortar businesses have been around for a long time and have developed well established procedures for others to follow. If you are opening a physical restaurant, there's a good chance you can easily find someone to help you navigate through your journey.

But what if your business is mobile and is set to operate in multiple areas, cities, counties and regions? In this case, there are fewer proven strategies and procedures to follow. The freedom to roam around with your business is definitely littered with challenges... most of which are unique to almost every truck. Being in a new place each and every day can wear on almost any food truck owner. From health codes to inventory management to budgets, you've got to have a strong will to survive in this type of business.

From the viewpoint of an outsider, the food truck business appears to be a lot of fun! And this is what is typically perceived by onlookers and customers thinking about starting their own food truck. What isn't necessarily visible on the surface is all the hard work that goes into getting the truck up and running, setting up a menu that is profitable, marketing, pricing, mechanical maintenance, adhering to regulations, staffing and much more!

Running your own food truck business requires more than just a passion for preparing and serving great food! It takes a lot of research and planning before a single penny is spent regarding the purchase of an actual food truck. Composing a detailed business plan is essential in the early stages. Even with a sound business plan in place, don't be surprised if things get more expensive than you originally budgeted in the startup phase. That is a sentiment shared by many food truck owners.

The Food Truck Owner's Handbook is designed to help prepare you on your journey of being a food truck business owner. The information in this book is designed to educate and inspire ideas so you can ask the right kinds of questions as you build your business. This is my contribution to future food truck owners and my love of seeing what's possible when it comes to mobile cuisine. These are definitely exciting times in the food truck industry and I'm always surprised at the concepts and innovation I see out on the streets! I wish you much success with your mobile food business!

-Andrew Moorehouse-

Chapter 1 - Food Trucks: Fad or Long-Term Business?

The food truck industry is rapidly growing and many people are cashing in on this small corner of the food and beverage sector. You've probably seen food trucks around lunch and dinner time serving food to long lines of hungry people. Now consider this, if every person you see standing in line is paying $12 to $20 each it's easy to quickly see how owning a food truck can be a lucrative business venture. But is this just a fad that will eventually go away? There is no crystal ball to look into the future but there are indicators that can help determine the sustainability of the food truck industry.

One sign that might classify this industry as a fad is the sudden creation of food truck related programming on television. Shows like Eat Street, Food Truck Face Off and Food Truck Paradise have really put food trucks into the spotlight and brought a lot of publicity to the industry. Among the most popular of these shows is The Food Network's Great Food Truck Race hosted by celebrity chef Tyler Florence. If you haven't seen it before, it's a contest where newbies to the food truck industry are put into various cooking and business challenges as they travel across the United States. The winner is determined by the amount of money they make each week. The grand prize winner wins $50,000 and their own food truck. Multiple seasons of The Great Food Truck Race have been shot and each season generates new buzz for the industry.

Eat Street on the other hand showcases several food trucks in each episode and shows viewers shots of delicious food. It's this kind of stuff that gets people excited about starting their own food truck. A lot of viewers believe they can prepare food just as good as they see on TV or locally in their own town.

The food truck craze was also the inspiration for a major motion picture. The movie "Chef" directed by Jon Favreau was a hit with many fans. A television sitcom called "Happy Endings" was also inspired by the food truck industry. So it's not hard to see that the media has definitely noticed the rise of the food truck business.

But what if these television programs suddenly went away? Would the food truck industry still grow and stick around? It would be conceivable that food trucks are here to stay. New food truck owners will enter and exit the industry but for the most part mobile food culture has become part of the new business landscape for entrepreneurs. It is inevitable that the industry will thin out a bit over time but will never completely go away. But just because a food truck business decides to shut its doors for good doesn't mean it's completely gone. The owner's may have decided to evolve to a brick-and-mortar restaurant or other related industry. Sometimes, the food truck is just the springboard for more growth in the future and brand building.

One of the most alluring features of starting a food truck is the low cost of entry. This is the main reason why so many people become mobile food entrepreneurs. It poses relatively lower risk than many other types of businesses. It also takes fewer people to run a food truck.

For some people, they might be starting a food truck business because they think they can jump in and make some quick cash. This could work but without long term planning and strategy, it would be extremely difficult to survive very long.

Research has shown that large sprawling cities that charge higher rent often have the largest number of food trucks. Part of that growth is the acceptance and favorable laws aimed at the food truck industry. But that growth can vary in different parts of the country. Cities with strong advocate groups are able to rally to help pass regulations and get city leaders to allow the industry to grow.

Some cities, no matter large or small still have outdated laws and regulations that severely inhibit the ability of the food truck industry to flourish in those areas. Food truck owners in those areas are struggling to catch up. Even so, it is estimated that the food truck industry is on track to become a $2.8 billion dollar industry by the year 2017. In the years from 2007 to 2012 the industry enjoyed a growth rate of 8.4%

Brick-and-mortar restaurant owners have definitely noticed the impact that food trucks have had on their business. So much so that some of these restaurant owners have lobbied hard to keep food trucks away from their establishments. But not all restaurant owners are so quick to try and restrict their mobile competition. Some have realized the business potential of successful food trucks and have even gone on and opened up their own to supplement their brick-and-mortar restaurants.

Not only do food trucks compete with brick-and-mortar restaurants, they are also competing strongly with traditional catering companies. Will food trucks eventually replace catering companies? Not likely but as you can see that the food truck industry is highly flexible and is extending itself to other areas of business other than just serving food curbside.

I believe the food truck industry is here to stay. It has become part of our foodie culture and is a great option for customers looking for new dining experiences. Food trucks and food carts have been around for a long time but the current iteration of the gourmet food truck has definitely marked its place in the entrepreneurial community. The low cost and the speed at which entrepreneurs can get up and running will keep this industry going for a long time to come.

Chapter 2 - Keeping Your Food Truck in Tip Top Shape

If you take care of your truck, it will take care of you! Regular and preventative maintenance is the key to making sure your truck is operational when you need it. If your truck is sitting in a garage or commissary parking lot with engine or equipment failure, you will be losing out on income every hour it is not on the streets serving customers. Maintenance is important all year round but if you continue to operate during the winter months especially in harsh climates, it is even more important to stay on top of it.

Having a reliable mechanic is invaluable and the expense is well worth it if you want to be able to open for business whenever you want to. Customers can be disappointed when you can't show up to a location where they're expecting you. If you're handy, you may be able to do some of the maintenance yourself and save valuable time and money.

However, if you're not familiar with step van maintenance then having the number to a trusty mechanic is the best advice. The same goes for equipment inside your truck. A lot of repairs can be done on your own but there are probably parts of your equipment that are better left to the professionals.

It's good practice to have your mechanic do an inspection at the beginning of the season especially if your truck has seen little use over the winter. This will help ensure that your truck is in great shape and ready for the crowds!

Like the car that you drive every day, there are things you can check yourself in order to keep things running smoothly. Here are a few things you should add to your maintenance schedule that you can do on your own or with your mechanic.

Change Your Engine Oil Regularly - If you've owned a car or motorcycle, you already know the importance of changing the oil on a regular basis. But how often you need to do it will depend on the type of vehicle you own. Step vans have different frequency requirements as well as using different types of oil than regular cars. The age of your truck will also need to be taken into consideration.

Your mechanic can help you figure out how often the engine oil needs to be changed in your food truck. Often we delay changing the oil in our personal vehicles but don't delay the oil change on your food truck. Obviously keeping the engine properly lubricated will help it to last longer.

Maintain and Inspect Tires - Everyone has experienced a flat tire and the inconvenience it causes. But when you get a flat tire on your food truck, it can cost you income especially if you can't make it to your venue. A flat tire doesn't necessarily mean you will miss out on a service but you will certainly be late... that is if you can get your tire repaired quickly.

You should inspect your tires regularly and monitor the air pressure. That way you know if there's a slow leak or problem and you can take care of it before you are in a critical situation. Driving with low air pressure can lead to reduced performance and handling on the road. It can also cause early tire wear. Of course you can't predict when you might run over a nail or something but regular inspections can uncover foreign objects lodged in your tires. Check your air pressure before you hit the road as part of your daily checklist before heading out to a service. That way you can air up with a portable pump or stop at a gas station.

Checking the Engine Battery - The battery in your food truck is what gives the starter the power to turn the engine to start. You don't want to be faced with a dead battery just as you've loaded up your truck and ready to roll. You know how frustrating and inconvenient it can be to have a dead battery on your own vehicle! Like other parts of your food truck, your mechanic can perform some basic tests to determine if you battery needs to be replaced.

In cold weather the battery has to work extra hard to crank the engine. But if you find that if your battery dies once or twice, get it replaced! Vehicle batteries are relatively inexpensive when compared to the income loss due to a truck that won't start. The battery is something you could swap out yourself. If you need help, ask your mechanic to show you how so you'll know how to do it the next time around.

Check Your Fluids - The fluids inside your food truck's engine need to be monitored so they don't run low. They also need to be replaced or refilled at regular intervals to make sure your engine is running at optimum performance. As part of your regular maintenance, schedule a thorough vehicle check in the beginning of spring and the winter. Also perform periodic checks every couple of weeks to be sure nothing is leaking.

Fluids like transmission oil, antifreeze, brake and power steering fluid are crucial to keep your food truck running smoothly and without problems. Again, some of these are things you could change or refill yourself. If you need help, consult with your mechanic and have him or her show you how to do it.

Checking Belts and Hoses - One more thing to add to your maintenance checklist is a regular inspection of your belts and hoses. The heat of the engine coupled with constant changing temperatures put a lot of strain on these parts. This heating up and cooling down can lead to excessive stretching or even breaking.

If you or your mechanic can see visible signs of wear on belts and hoses, it's best to change them out before problems happen. These types of repairs are fairly inexpensive and will keep your truck in excellent running condition.

Staying on top of maintenance needs to be one of the top items in your priority list among all the other high-priority items that go along with running a gourmet food truck. One of the worst things that can happen on a business day is being stranded on the side of the road or stuck at your home base because of mechanical or equipment problems. Most of this can be preventable with periodic checks of the systems on your truck. Be sure to get tips from your mechanic so you can be a well-informed food truck owner.

It's also a good idea to share maintenance procedures with members of your staff so that there is more than one person that knows how to troubleshoot problems when they arise. Your food truck is the key piece of equipment to generating your income. Treat it with care and it will be a reliable partner as you continue to grow your business.

Chapter 3 - Creating Amazing Customer Experiences

While preparing good food is a key ingredient for a successful food truck business, caring for your customers is just as important if not more important! If you can create raving fans that are passionate about your business you'll essentially have evangelists that will recommend your food and help spread the word about your services.

There are no set ways to care for your customers or gain their loyalty but there are things you can do to make their experience at your truck a great and memorable one. Building relationships with your customers can be very tough when the only time you have to interact with them is during the ordering and food preparation process. This is especially difficult to do when you're trying to maximize the number of customers that place orders and pay for your food. But even though your food and revenues are what keep you in business, you really need good customers to help you achieve your goals.

Visiting a food truck is really an experience like no other type of dining experience. You need to make that experience an enjoyable one not only for your customer's tummies but also in their minds. They want the whole experience to meet or exceed their expectations. There still exists a novelty surrounding the whole food truck scene but if you can let your passion shine from the moment a customer locks eyes on your truck to their very last bite, you'll create a great long lasting impression.

Subtle Yet Very Effective Customer Service Tips

For most food truck owners, the foundations of great customer service are already in place but like with most things, they can always be refined. Small tweaks can make a huge difference even if they aren't blatant changes. The following suggestions are all designed to create the best possible experience for your customers.

Greet Walk Up Customers With Enthusiasm - When a potential customer passes by your truck, one of the first things they do is look at the menu and the food that people are walking away with. When you see a potential customer examining what you have to offer, be sure to greet them even if you don't know if they're going to purchase from you or not. A simple interaction to get them to learn more about your food can get them to try it. Start with something like *"How are you doing today?"* or *"Welcome to [your food truck name] let me know if you have any questions"* or *"You guys look hungry, would you like to try our [amazing dish]? It's made with 100% grass-fed beef"*. I'm sure you get the idea. Just be friendly and welcoming.

If you recognize a returning customer, definitely acknowledge that you know that they have been to your truck in the past. Ask if they want to try something different or let them know what your specials are for the day. General questions like *"How's your day been?"* or *"Back for lunch again?"* also help spur up conversation and perhaps another sale.

Have a Clear Menu Posted - The items on your menu are what people are most curious about when they visit your truck. So it needs to be clear and readable. Use larger fonts or handwriting if there's enough space. It's best practice to include the name of the item, a short description and a clearly marked price. If you have special features about a dish like gluten free or no-hormones for example, include that in the description as additional selling points.

TORTA $8

TAX INCLUDED IN PRICE

Field Roast chipotle sausage, avocado spread slaw mix (CABBAGE, CARROTS, BRUSSEL SPROUTS, KALE), house-made chipotle crema house-pickled red onion on a telera roll

$5 DEAL!
2 TACOS OF CHOICE!

Your menu should be placed or mounted where people can see it even if there's a crowd around the truck. At food truck festivals, many people peruse their choices before purchasing and the menu is the first thing they look at. If you operate into the evening hours, be sure to have some lighting on your menu. Small spotlights can easily be mounted to the exterior of your food truck that highlights the menu.

Some menus are printed while others are handwritten on a chalkboard or dry erase board. Depending on how often your menu changes, handwritten menu boards may be the best option. As the end of the service period nears the end, you may end up running out of ingredients for certain menu items. When you stop offering an item, be sure to indicate that on the menu so people know what to expect. Handwritten menus can have items easily erased or crossed out. For printed menu boards, I've seen some food truck owners use blue painter's tape to cross out items that are no longer available. One truck I saw had their menu printed on magnetic strips that attached to the side of the truck. As the day went on, they were able to easily remove the magnetic strips one by one as they discontinued certain menu items.

If you're using digital menu boards, be sure that they are shaded during the day so that they are still readable on sunny days. Digital menu boards offer the most flexibility but they suffer from daylight glare and possible malfunction. Obviously at night, these electronic flat screen menus are very readable but they require extra equipment to be mounted into an otherwise already cramped truck interior.

Separate Your Customer Interaction Areas- Even though the crowd surrounding a popular food truck can look chaotic, there can be order to the madness! Many trucks have customers order and pick up their food at the same service window. This is an effective technique for a lot of food truck owners. You can make it easier for your customers to understand the ordering and pickup process if you separate your customers into two groups. Have them form one line that is for ordering and another line or area for people to pick up their food.

One of the most effective ways to do this is to have a staff member take orders and make payments at the passenger door of your truck. Some will also have a little table set up near the front of the truck for payment processing equipment. Once you've taken an order, you can move that customer off to the main service window to wait for their order to come up. This way, when people walk up to your truck, they'll know where to stand and it helps keep the crowd organized as much as it can be.

Offer Easy Payment Choices and Options - Food truck owners love it when cash comes in. Customers love it when they have choices of payments. Cash is always best but not many people carry enough cash around these days to pay for everything on a day-to-day basis. So in addition to cash, you'll need a reliable credit card payment system that is easy for customers to use.

Most mobile payment systems have easy guided instructions for the customer to follow during the transaction process. To avoid delays or other technical issues, it may be a good idea to have accounts with more than one brand of payment system. Imagine if you only had one of the systems and for some reason, a data connection was lost or you weren't able to log into it. You wouldn't be able to take any credit card payments until the system was back online.

If your system is down, you'd have to turn away all those customers who can only pay by credit card. This means the customer can't experience your food and you'll lose out on potential income until the problem is sorted out. So having two or more mobile payment systems on-board should provide you enough of a back up to keep your food truck operating smoothly with no impact on your customers.

Accommodating Special Requests - This little tip can be annoying at times but it really helps make the customer happy as long as they're reasonable. Sometimes customers will make special requests with their orders. They'll ask for things like "no onion" or "extra pickles" or "no bun". These may seem simple but sometimes they can be a pain to provide because of the number of orders to keep track of. However, keeping the customer happy is of utmost importance.

If you find a pattern of continued requests, you might decide to make slight adjustments to your menu. Or another solution is to charge a very small fee for modifications to the menu items. However, don't make it seem like you're punishing the customer just because they don't like onions or other ingredients in the dish. They're just trying to get their meal just the way they like it and they'll keep coming back if they feel they've been taken care of.

Clearly Call Out Completed Orders - Public areas are noisy especially near a busy street or festival. So when a customer's food is ready, you want make sure your customer knows it. Most trucks take a name during an order or maybe even a number (which is less common). To make the final interaction with the customer a good one, make sure to call out their name or order number loudly and clearly. With a lot of people milling around the truck and all the other voices going on at the same time, customers can get nervous about knowing when their order is ready.

So be ready to take a deep breath and get some force behind your voice when you call their name. Perhaps you have an employee with a voice that clearly cuts through the noise. We've all heard people with those kinds of voices, right? But the main thing to remember is to make the customer feel at ease when their food is ready for pick up.

Some food truck owners use a public address or PA system to call out names. This can help if you don't feel like your voice can carry beyond the noise or you just don't want to have to shout out names all day. The PA system utilizes an exterior mounted speaker and allows you to use your regular conversation voice levels. Be sure to have the volume up high enough for the people around your truck to hear it but not so loud that it becomes annoying and bothersome to people and trucks in the vicinity.

Keep Condiments Well-Stocked Near Your Truck - When your customers receive their food, your interaction with them is not quite finished yet. Your customers will need napkins and most are expecting to add something to their food in the form of condiments. Whether it's salsa, ketchup, mustard or the must-have favorite, Sriracha sauce, you'll need these items on-hand and available for your customers.

Customers become accustomed to eating their favorite foods along with their favorite condiments. If the condiment is missing, then their experience won't be quite as enjoyable. Condiments are sometimes placed on a built-in shelf just below the service window. This is a great place for them but can sometimes hold up the pickup process if others are waiting for their food. Other food truck owners set up a small table just to the side of the service window to free up the area where customers pick up their food.

Your condiment table or shelf should be closely monitored so you can replenish the items that are running low or have run out. Heaven forbid that you run out of Sriracha! So every ten minutes or so when you peek your head out of the window, check to see how much of your condiments have been used.

Keep an eye on your napkins as well. There's nothing more annoying to customers than grabbing their food only to find there are no napkins available. If possible use a napkin dispenser to help reduce the amount of napkins that customers will swipe. Select a dispenser that only allows one napkin at a time. Otherwise, customers will grab more than they need and you'll end up running out faster. If you don't have a napkin holder, remember to place a weighted object on top of your pile of napkins so they don't blow away.

Chapter 4 - Relationships That Help Build Your Business

The food truck community is generally very passionate and supportive of each other. Anyone who owns a food truck knows the hard work that went into getting to where they're at. Ask any food truck owner for assistance and you're bound to get helpful expert advice. Cultivating relationships within the industry can produce great benefits. Becoming involved with food truck organizations and individual food truck owners can lead to long-term relationships that can help you throughout your professional career.

Be Considerate of Other People's Time

While food truck owners are generally very nice people who are willing to give you assistance, you should be mindful that they too have busy lives with schedules and issues within their own lives and businesses. Don't take advantage of their kindness and take up too much of their time.

When you do meet up, you should have clearly defined topics you want to discuss in order to be as productive as possible with the time they've made available to you. And if you're asked for advice, be sure to reciprocate the kindness that others have offered you. It's this willingness to share that makes the food truck industry such a friendly and supportive community. Most large cities have at least one food truck organization that promotes and advocates the growth of mobile businesses. Getting involved with one of these groups early on (even in the startup stage of your food truck) can help you stay current with local legislation and regulations. Often these groups consist of

other food truck owners, city officials and other groups who want to see the food truck industry prosper in their area.

Advantages of Food Truck Groups

When you become part of an active food truck organization in your area, your resource base opens up immediately. You can get tips on getting an awesome commissary at a great price, access to graphic designers who have experience with other mobile food businesses, contacts with banking institutions, preferred treatment at events and more!

Being a part of these organizations is a two-way street. You need to contribute to the organization and their members also. There are always going to be other food truck owners that need your support so help them out and be an active member of a tight-knit support group.

Numerous business opportunities could become available to you with these groups. Some of them may even actively organize food truck events or block out areas where they have negotiated permission for trucks to park and conduct business. If you are invited to the events they have sponsored or organized, don't forget to thank them for the opportunity. Remember to post updates and photos to your social media accounts with links back to their websites or social media accounts.

In addition, personally thank the organizers for their hard work and giving you the opportunity to be a part of it. The organization and its members are all in it for the prosperity of everyone involved.

A Real-World Partnership Example

In Seattle's Greenwood neighborhood, one such partnership I've noticed involves a symbiotic pairing between a beer pub and local food trucks. Chuck's Hop Shop is an incredibly popular neighborhood hangout especially during nice summer days on their outdoor patio. They have 30+ rotating beers on tap and a plethora of 1000+ bottled brews for their customers to choose from. As far as food goes, they offer limited snacks and ice cream from their establishment.

But that's where the partnership begins. They bring in a different food trucks 7 days a week to serve their customers. On the weekends (including some Fridays) they rotate 2 different trucks a day. This allows Chuck's Hop Shop to focus on what they do best which is beer and they let the food trucks provide the meals. For Chuck's, it means customers may stay longer to order additional brews and these on-site food trucks enjoy the extra opportunity to make more money.

For marketing, Chuck's posts a schedule on their website of each truck that will be visiting on each day of the week. And for most of these food trucks, Chuck's is a regular weekly location and familiar customer base they can depend on.

However, you may not find a business exactly like this to partner with in your city but there are definitely opportunities similar to this. Feel free to talk to the owners of businesses that you think have potential for a good partnership. You never know unless you ask. You'll probably get a lot of rejections but eventually one or more opportunities could present itself that will help make your efforts pay off.

Other Examples

Strategic partnership examples occur everywhere and you may not even be aware of them. The next examples aren't food truck related but it could help exercise your mind and thinking who or what types of businesses you could possibly partner with. These partnerships help both businesses involved and provide customers with convenient access to services. For example, Starbucks often partners with grocery stores where the grocery store dedicates a space for the coffee company to sell their coffee. This provides convenience because shoppers can get everything on their grocery list plus a cup of their favorite mocha in one stop.

Another great example is the partnerships that Microsoft has with Dell, HP and many other PC manufacturers. The PC companies build the hardware but need software from Microsoft to run them. This example is a little different than non-tech based businesses but you can see how one business operates with the other and helps generate a large base of customers for both.

Same goes for wedding photographers and wedding venues. If there's a wedding, usually a photographer is involved. If a photographer is partnered with a popular venue, then they may get more recommendations and in turn generate more business than they would without the partnership. The venue coordinators most-likely get asked the question of a recommending a photographer so it benefits the venue to have a name on-hand to tell their clients.

By partnering with another company, you can more easily extend your reach and increase your exposure to markets and customers you would normally not have access to. For food truck owners, finding a business that needs food is really one of the best opportunities you can find. High school sports, outdoor theaters, festivals, grand openings and art walks are just some of the ideas you can pursue.

Chapter 5 - How Much Money Can Food Trucks Make

One of the biggest questions asked when starting a food truck is "How much money can a food truck make?" While there is no definite answer to this question, we can explore the possibilities and get estimates about the amount of revenue that can be generated by a food truck business.

The food truck industry covers a wide sector from the classic catering trucks seen at construction sites to the modern gourmet food trucks of today. In this book we are mainly focused on today's gourmet food trucks which offer unique dining experiences for customers. Given that some of these food trucks can prepare and serve food that is superior in quality to some high-end restaurants, the income potential can be promising.

According to the Intuit Financial Network, food trucks are on track to become a $2.7 billion dollar industry by 2017. That is almost quadruple the amount from estimates made in 2012.

The food truck industry is constantly evolving with new and innovative ways of marketing. Social networking has definitely been part of the explosive growth of the food truck industry and it shows no signs of slowing down. In the beginning, accepting cash was the only method of monetary transactions when doing business on the streets. But as the industry grew, the need for mobile credit card payment systems was born.

Today, if you plan on opening food truck, you will need to establish a way to accept multiple forms of payments from your customers. If you only accept cash, you will severely limit the number of customers that can buy food from your truck. Plus it can be Inconvenient or cause problems for both you and your customer. Have you ever walked into a food establishment, ordered food and then found out they only accept cash? You then reach into your pocket to find you don't have enough cash because you mostly pay with credit cards! How does that make you feel? It's an awkward situation for both parties involved.

But with current innovations in financial technology, mobile payment apps and portable credit card readers are now readily available for any type of business. As a food truck owner, you can now accept almost any of credit card wherever you go! These untethered Point-of-Sale systems or POS are how the majority of payments are made in the food truck industry today. If you own a smartphone or tablet device, you can get set up and accept payments very quickly. Before moving onto the question of how much money can a food truck make, let's take a brief look at how money actually goes from the customer and into your bank account.

Where to Get a Portable Credit Card Reader

Accepting credit cards from customers is essential when it comes to running a food truck. In fact the majority of the revenue you report will come from credit card purchases. And now it's easier than ever to get your truck set up to accept credit card payments. Portable credit card payment systems are available from a number of companies. Some are run by companies you've heard of but a few are new to the industry and run on their own proprietary systems. There are even payment systems that can tie into popular accounting software.

You don't have to look far to get your hands on a fully functioning system and most of them are free or available at a very low cost. When I say low cost I mean $20 USD or less. Most of the systems consist of a tiny card reader that you plug into the headphone jack of your mobile phone or tablet. Once your account is set up, swiping credit cards and accepting payments is easy.

You can order these handy credit card readers online and they're usually free but the ones offered by major financial institutions can also be found in local stores like Walgreens, Walmart, Target and others. If you pick one up at a local retail store, be prepared to pay a small fee but you'll be refunded the cost to you once your account is set up.

Brands of Credit Card Readers

Many companies are jumping on-board to provide mobile payment services. This is just a brief overview of the top choices in the industry. Each provider has different fee structures so you definitely need to look into the fine print so you know how much you're being charged to use their services. Here are a few of the portable payment systems to consider.

PayPal Here - You have probably heard of PayPal and their system of processing payments for online purchases. So it makes sense that they have built a mobile system that makes accepting credit card payments a snap. PayPal Here requires a PayPal account and we recommend signing up for a separate business account if you don't already have one.

Square - Founded by Jack Dorsey (the creator of Twitter). Square was one of the first mobile payment systems that utilized mobile devices like phones and tablets as the point-of-sale. One of the highlights of this system is that you can set up favorites for 125 of your most popular items. This allows for quicker checkout for your customers and helps improve your efficiency.

Intuit GoPayment - As one of the leaders of accounting software, Intuit has developed a system that integrates right into their popular QuickBooks software. Customer receipts are completely customizable using your food truck logo and business contact information. You can also offer to send receipts via email or text.

PayAnywhere - Created by North American Bancard, PayAnywhere is another major player in mobile payment processing. They offer 24 hour 7 days a week support should you have any issues with their services. GoPayment also integrates seamlessly with QuickBooks making accounting tasks easier to do.

All these systems are easy to use and you can try them out for a very low cost. It's easy to switch between the different payment systems plus it's a good idea to have a backup in case one of the providers goes offline for any reason. For the food truck industry any of the choices listed above can provide excellent service for you and your customers.

How Much Money Can You Realistically Make?

According to professionals in financial institutions, some have reported seeing gourmet food trucks generating over $50,000 a month in credit card transactions alone each month. That figure does not include cash transactions. But if you estimate that another third of the income generated was the result of cash payments, that monthly figure could be up by another $15,000.

Of course no figures are completely accurate unless you actually see the accounting behind a food truck business. With that said, the following are revenue estimates for the 3 major categories of mobile food found on the streets today.

Gourmet Food Truck - $20,000 to $65,000 a month
Lunch Catering Truck - $6,000 to $14,000 a month
Simple Food Cart - $5,000 to $16,000 a month

32

Obviously food costs, salaries and other expenses are going to affect the bottom line. But research shows that brick and mortar restaurants can report profit margins of 5% to 7%. Food trucks on the other hand have reported profit margins of 10% to 15%.

Top earning food trucks can bring in $780,000 per year. However, an average gourmet food truck could expect revenues around $240,000 per year.

Other factors that can severely affect revenue numbers are:

Time of year
Time of day
Marketing efforts
Local population
Type of food
Maintenance
Locations
Equipment failure
Etc.

Maximizing foot traffic is one of the keys to profitability. That's why groups in many cities have opened up food truck pods. These are semi-permanent locations that can host a group of food trucks at one time. Some of these pods are smaller with 5 to 6 trucks while others can be much larger. As an example of how these groupings can help revenues, San Francisco's Off The Grid "Night Market" has been advantageous for its food truck partners.

Typical revenues for food trucks participating in the Off The Grid events can bring in $250,000 to $500,000. The top food trucks operating at this venue can bring in close to $1,000,000.

In addition to generating revenue on the streets, most food truck owners have pursued alternate forms of business using the resources they have available on hand. This usually comes in the form of catering for businesses and private events such as weddings and parties. Food trucks have an advantage over traditional catering companies in that food trucks offer exciting new options when it comes to dining. Some food truck owners mention that their catering events are their most profitable activities.

Most food truck businesses already have access to the same types of facilities that catering companies have so it makes perfect business sense to also offer catering as part of your business plan. With catering, you can predict more accurately your costs and profitability because you'll know the size of audience you will be serving. And often, catering customers are willing to pay a higher price.

Chapter 6 - Commissary and Kitchen Requirements

Did you know that there are strict laws and regulations regarding overnight storage of your food truck? The most common facility for food truck owners to park their truck is at a commissary. The commissary is the place where you are required to park your vehicle when not in use.

Commissaries can also be commercial kitchens. The reason why commissaries and commercial kitchens are required is that they help keep this industry in-check and promotes overall food safety. As a food truck owner, you will be spending a great deal time working inside your truck. However you're more-likely to spend an even greater amount time working in a commissary or commercial kitchen. The primary reason you need the services of a commissary is that it is illegal to prepare food you're going sell from your home. Your food truck and commissary will need to be officially approved and needs to operate within the guidelines of local health codes.

Health inspectors will also check that you are using an approved commissary or commercial kitchen. Their main job is to make sure that your food is stored and handled safely whether it's inside your truck or at a commissary. Any violations can cost you time and money.

If you are already a restaurant owner, then you already have a commercial kitchen at your disposal. For those who don't, a commercial kitchen or commissary will need to be added to your list of expenses.

SHORE POWER
240 VOLT 4 WIRE
50 AMP ONLY

Costs of Commercial Kitchens

Commercial kitchens make their money by charging a monthly fee for you to use them but there are creative ways that can help you reduce your costs when it comes to renting a commissary. Commissaries usually charge a monthly fee with average costs that could run you $800 to $1200 per month. This rate varies highly because each commissary offers different types of services. If cost is an issue, a simple way to reduce expenses is to partner with and share a commercial kitchen space with another business. This way, you can split the cost of the monthly fees.

Some facilities can be bare-bones while others may include security cameras, round the clock security staff, electricity, fuel or other necessary supplies. One of the requirements needed before renting a kitchen is liability insurance; however, each commercial kitchen or commissary will undoubtedly have additional requirements that are unique to each location. Just be sure to get all the specifics before signing a contract. If you have trouble finding an affordable commissary, there are some other options you should consider.

Commissary Alternatives

Local schools, churches or other venues may have a certified commercial kitchen that you can rent. Additional options can include hospitals, firehouses, and even catering facilities that already house the types of equipment that you will need. If you decide to go with one of these alternatives, you will most-likely have to coordinate the use times with the kitchen owners or other users. And it's important to understand that you may only have access to these facilities early in the morning or late at night. Depending on your menu and operation times, this might not be the best option for you. But with a little creativity, you can potentially uncover a great deal on a kitchen rental.

If you've located a commercial kitchen you want to rent, make sure everything is legal and the contract is in writing. That way both parties know what to expect in case issues arise. Having your lawyer look over the contract is also advisable. The various rules surrounding commercial kitchens exist to protect the consumer and to promote safety for the food truck industry. You should never place your food truck business at risk by taking shortcuts when comes to cleanliness.

Services Offered By Commissaries

A commissary or commercial kitchen is essential for a food truck business to fully operate. They offer services that a food truck owner needs to follow regulations and laws. Not only do you prepare food at a commissary, but there are a host of other daily activities that are performed there.

Convenient Access to Supplies - A well-equipped commissary will have the most essential supplies on-hand that you can get access to in a pinch. So rather than having to rush to a store to purchase items that you need, you can easily get them at the commissary. The time savings can be huge when things are busy... and when are they not? However, you'll have to check on the fine print on your contract because there may be certain services you are required to pay for when you are based out of a particular facility.

On-Site Storage - One of the big benefits of a commissary is that you can get on-site storage of your ingredients and supplies. Commissaries are fully licensed and approved for commercial food storage. Depending on the amount of storage you have agreed upon at the facility, you can stock up and save money by buying some of your supplies in bulk without having to worry about where you're going to store it all.

On-Site Parking - Another benefit to a commissary is that you can park your food truck at the facility. It's not just a convenient place to park but it is also where you are legally required to store your truck at night. Remember you cannot park your food truck at your home.

Charging Stations - During your service hours, your truck is most-likely going to run off generator power. But when you park overnight, you will want to connect your vehicle to shore power to keep batteries charged or refrigeration equipment running. Your commissary should have adequate connections to keep your truck plugged in. The cost of the power could be included in your rent or may be charged separately for actual power usage.

Cleaning and Waste Disposal - Another important feature of a commissary is the cleaning and waste disposal facilities. After a food service, typically a truck will return to a commissary where cooking tools and equipment can be cleaned. There are strict rules regarding how often certain surfaces and equipment need to be cleaned. Your commissary will help you stay within regulations and avoid any violations.

Waste water requires special disposal facilities because it contains grease and food particles that cannot be dumped into regular drains. Any used water and solid waste needs to be disposed of at the facility. Heavy fines can be imposed if disposal regulations are not followed.

Vehicle Maintenance - Time is money and it's never a good time when your truck needs maintenance work. However, many commissaries offer mechanics services on-site. If your commissary provides mechanical services, routine maintenance becomes a whole lot easier. Other services can include kitchen equipment repair, routine inspections and other necessary work.

Your commissary is your partner as you work in the food truck industry. It is also a place where you can interact with other food truck owners who are working in close quarters with you on a daily basis. Not only are you part of the larger food truck community in your area, but you become part of a smaller more intimate group at the commissary. Sharing ideas and getting help is a lot easier when you've got the support group to back you up.

Chapter 7 - From Business Owner to Employer

Running a food truck requires a lot of time commitment! Food truck owners start their day long before their first service starts. The day often begins with ingredient shopping, food preparation, social media updates, mechanical inspections and more. The end of the day is also filled with work that could extend several hours after the last customer is served. This leaves very little time for anything else. If the number of hours sounds overwhelming then it is time to hire additional help. In the beginning you may be doing everything yourself. And depending on the level of complexity of your food truck business, you may or may not need to hire additional hands to help out with daily operations. Many trucks operate with just the owners while just as many if not more have additional staff members to help out with various tasks. The owners may even run one service at a location themselves and then have staff members in charge at a different location during the day.

There is a definitely a benefit to having employees on your staff. The extra expense can be worth it so you don't burn yourself out. One of the first things you should consider is how many hours of work is required each day. As mentioned earlier, you need to include the hours of work prior to and after your actual service hours. For example, if you are open for business from 10am to 6pm, that equates to about a 60 hour work week if you are open 7 days a week. That's not including the time spent before and after you open for business. If you add a minimum of 2 hours before and after your service hours, you're looking at almost 85 hours of work each week. That's more than twice the amount of hours most people work at a regular job!

Add to those times any additional hours where you might stay open later or attend special events like catering parties and your work week really starts to get over the top with the number of hours you need to put in. It could be that you only need additional help during these special events. Larger services like events and catering requires more preparation time and extra hands during the event. You will also be spending time meeting with your clients and venue representative as you map out your game plan for a successful event.

Some food trucks can operate with as little as 2 people on board and still handle a large volume of customers. But that depends on your menu. If your menu features foods that are simple to prepare and assemble then a couple of people can probably manage the volume. Gourmet ice cream, donut and grilled cheese trucks for example can be well-suited for smaller staff operations. At minimum you will need someone who can cook and someone who can take orders plus other side duties.

How Much of Your Time is Required?

There's nothing wrong with long hours and hard work but there comes a point when it stops being fun. So you need to come to terms with how many hours you actually want to spend in the truck or doing other business related tasks. This is when you need to determine the types of tasks you want to do most or have the most expertise in. Do you enjoy cooking or talking to customers? Do you thrive with the backend business and marketing part of your operations? It's good to be aware of the tasks that is better spent with your own time and hiring employees to complete the work that can easily be done by others. That way, you can spend more time building your business than running daily operations. There's a big distinction between working in your truck and working on your food truck business.

What tasks can help you make the most revenue for your mobile food business? Your time might be better spent meeting with clients and booking special events like catering rather than preparing food inside the kitchen.

You Don't Necessarily Need Full Time Employees

Sometimes food truck owners can handle the workweek on their own without additional staff. But there are moments when taking on additional help can make your operations smoother. If you know there is an event or service where you know there is going to be an exceptional volume of customers, then you can just hire temporary help during those events.

The good thing is that the people you hire don't necessarily have to have experience in the food or restaurant industry. They can all be taught on the job as they work their way up to higher positions. Of course experience working in a fast-paced environment and food service does help.

Job Duties for Your Employees

While there is probably not necessarily one specific job that an employee will be asked to do, I will try to list some of the duties you will ask your new hire to do. The work varies and everyone has to help out in some way to ensure that the operations go smoothly during a service.

Depending on experience, a new hire will typically start as an order taker. Greeting customers and sending orders through to the kitchen is a job most people can do. This is often the best way to train new employees so they can get familiar the workflow of your truck. From there, an employee can move to the prep table where sauces and other finishing touches are added to dishes before they are handed to the customer.

The job that really dictates the workflow of the truck is the chef or person in charge of actually cooking the food. That could be the person working on a grill, fryer, crepe iron or other piece of equipment. Order tickets go to the chef where the whole cooking and preparation process starts.

Key Role of the Chef

The efficiency of the whole operation rests on the hands of the chef or the person in charge of cooking and prepping the main food items. They are the ones that get the meats and vegetables prepped before service. They are the ones that monitor the orders coming in and pace the flow of the food heading out.

This person needs to be organized and be able to manage many things going on at one time. Different dishes require different prep times. This can prove to be a challenge even for the most experienced chef. Long lines and special requests can put added pressure on the one in charge of the kitchen.

Scheduling Employees and Pay Rates

Food truck employees aren't the highest paid workers but it's a good way to earn some income or just extra cash. Typical starting pay for a food truck employee is $8.00 an hour. Once your employee gets more experience and moves into a cooking position, rates can be $10.00 or more. On top of that, your employees can enjoy a bit extra from tips generated from each service location.

One of the side benefits for your employees is that you could offer them free food at the end of each shift. If you're friends with other trucks, you might share meals between the other trucks at the end of a service. This is easy to do if you are grouped together so workers and owners can bond and sample what everyone has to offer.

Food trucks typically operate 2 to 3 services a day. That means breakfast, lunch and dinner. A service can last 3 to 6 hours depending on the location and type of event. Commonly, the time spent actually cooking and serving food will be about 3 to 4 hours. Don't forget the additional hours spent preparing for the service and cleanup afterwards.

Some trucks can serve up to 150 orders or more per service. That means in a 4 hour service, food is ordered, cooked and served to a customer every 90 seconds. Add to that modified orders, customer complaints and mixed up orders, the work experience can be very hectic to say the least. So it does help to hire employees that can handle these high-pressure situations.

Chapter 8 - Passing Health Inspection with Flying Colors

Running a food truck requires that you adhere to local laws and regulations. However, long before rolling down the street for business, food truck vehicles and kitchens need to be approved for operations. That means that your truck is not road ready until your kitchen has passed initial health and safety tests. This should be of no surprise because every food establishment has to be inspected before it is approved to serve meals to customers.

But just because you're mobile doesn't mean that the inspections end there. Gourmet food trucks must undergo surprise health inspections usually at the most inopportune time. If you've ever owned or worked in a restaurant, you know that health inspectors will just show up out of the blue.

And because of the fast paced workflow of food truck businesses, the mere mention of a health inspector can put added pressure on an already stressful workday. The anxiety felt when a health inspector shows up is common and you shouldn't feel like you're being singled out. However, there are things you can do on a regular basis that will help you pass an inspection with less stress of failing.

There can be several mandatory health inspections throughout the year. You must adhere to the rules to make ensure that your food truck doesn't violate any health codes. In the United States alone, there are over 2,000 state and local organizations responsible for keeping tabs on food trucks.

Some of the most basic regulations require that gourmet food trucks have both hot and cold running water, a temperature controlled refrigerator, and a way to dispose of solid waste as well as wastewater.

As of now, there aren't necessarily universal standards for food trucks so it's best to check with your state and local laws specific to your area. Industry leaders believe that there may soon be a standardized checklist for all food trucks to follow no matter where they operate.

The best practice is to come up with a cleaning schedule and post these procedures visible for all staff to see so the task is easily manageable. Once an inspector arrives at your truck, it's too late to clean up! The last thing you want is to be shut down. Just one shutdown could really hurt your brand and reputation.

Preparing a Self-Inspection

One of the things you can do to be ready for the health inspector is to perform your own self-inspection at regular intervals. There is a slight chance that a health inspector will give notice when they will visit your truck but chances are most visits will come unannounced. So it's best to always be ready for the dreaded health inspector!

Here are some of the top things you should be looking for when you are inspecting your own food truck.

Food and Supplies - This includes all your raw ingredients, food preparation areas and food storage systems. You want to make sure all the food you have onboard is clean and safe for your customers to consume. Inspectors will check to make sure all your food is stored at the correct temperatures, especially those items that need to be kept cool.

Raw meat needs to be kept away and not touching foods that have already been cooked or raw ingredients. This can lead to cross-contamination and is a major problem if the inspector finds this issue. Be sure that foods aren't left out for long periods of time especially if they need to stay at certain temperatures.

If you store foods in containers, be sure to label and date them so you know when to dispose of them. Unused containers need to be cleaned and sanitized. These containers also need to be kept in a clean area until ready for use.

Cooking Equipment - As mentioned in the previous section, cooling units like refrigerators and freezers need to be kept at the correct temperatures. There should be thermometers either on the inside or temperature display mounted to the exterior of these appliances. This is an area the health inspector will focus on because it directly relates to the safety of the food you are selling.

Inspectors will also take a look at your plumbing system. Your fresh water tanks must be cleaned and sanitized on a regular basis to avoid contamination and foodborne illness. Water tanks in food trucks are meant to be used over a short period of time which means they must be emptied and refilled regularly to help prevent standing water and bacteria growth.

There must be a dedicated sink for hand washing along with soap. Your dishwashing water needs to be at the correct temperature for proper cleaning. Commercial sinks have 3 compartments and the first sink with the detergent must be at 110 degrees. If you are sanitizing with only water in the third compartment, the temperature in that sink needs to be 180+ degrees. Of course check with your local regulations in case they are different than what is presented here.

Your truck must have adequate ventilation and the proper equipment to move air inside your truck. Cleaning products must be kept away from any foods and you must employ a commercial kitchen or commissary for any type of food preparation that is not allowed onboard your vehicle.

Sanitary Conditions - When it comes to food preparation, all cooking and preparation surfaces must be clean and sanitized. There should be no signs of pests inside your truck. Your floors and countertops need to be cleaned daily to avoid build-up.

You must also have proper methods to dispose of your garbage both inside and outside the vehicle. In your sink, if any compartments get too saturated with food or detergent levels run low, they must be changed and refilled to proper temperatures. Used dishes and cooking tools need to be kept away from clean serving containers or dishes. And lastly, make sure countertops, floors and sinks are in good condition.

Required Paperwork On-Hand - You may also be asked to present the legal operating paperwork for your food truck. This means having all licenses up to date with the proper permits for operations. This may include the license and registration to the vehicle itself. The inspector may ask for a schedule of your cleaning routines and a visual inspection of the cleaning products you use. Hand washing posters should be posted above the hand washing sink.

What Else Will The Inspector Look For?

The inspector will most-likely check to see if your employees are following proper hand washing procedures. They will also be observing whether employees can answer questions about proper food and cleaning practices. Employees must be wearing proper attire and protective gear if necessary.

If you do your own self-inspection once or twice a week, you should be well prepared for when the health inspector suddenly shows up at your truck. Even though you may be in different locations every day, they will be able to find you the same way your customers find you. Eventually they will locate you for your inspection!

Chapter 9 - How to Make Real Money on the Side

Many food truck owners have come to the harsh reality that doing business on the streets just doesn't provide enough revenue to sustain an existence. It's a sad reality but a lot of food trucks have to find additional sources of revenue in order to remain profitable and survive.

One of the ways food truck owners have tapped into additional revenue streams is by offering catering services. Finding events to cater is a very effective way to make use of the resources you already own to grow your income. This is particularly a smart business practice during the quieter months where business often slows down. Usually this happens in the winter but that doesn't mean you can't do catering year-round.

One thing to remember is that catering is a well-established industry and it is very competitive so you need to figure out where you fit in the best. Not every event is going to be well suited for a food truck but there are many that would be a natural fit! But you need to be able to provide services just as good if not better than the traditional catering companies. That means you have the ability to service different capacities and have the equipment and staffing needed to successfully cater an event.

Before You Start Catering Services

Even though catering services is a great extension to your food truck business, there are some considerations you need to think about. The workflow is going to be entirely different than a regular service on the streets. You may need to revisit your business plan and train your staff for the additional workload and procedures. New permits and licenses may also be required before your first catering appointment.

Catering events will require that you review and thoroughly understand the requirements of offering a catering service in your area. Chances are that you already have the proper things in place to start but check local regulations in case you need additional permits. Your local health department or chamber of commerce is a great starting point for these conversations. Talking to other food truck owners and mobile food organizations is also a smart way to begin. You may want to talk directly with different venues where you want to offer your catering services. They'll also offer you requirements before you can even show up on their grounds.

Where Do You Want To Cater?

After you've had some initial conversations and figured out whether you need additional permits, it's time to start thinking of the different types of venues that could be suited for your truck. There are many corporate events and private parties that you could offer your services. You may want to try to service various types of events or you could focus and specialize in certain themed events only.

Either strategy can work but make sure it works with your business plan and the direction you want your business to be headed. Here are some of the events you could consider for catering.

Company Retreats
Weddings
Bridal Showers
Birthday Parties
Company Lunches
Seminars

Fundraisers
Sporting Events
Bar Mitzvahs
Bat Mitzvahs
Graduation Parties
Rehearsal Dinners
Block Parties
Backstage Concerts
Movie Sets
Parent/Teacher Conferences
Retirement Parties
Product Launch Events
Grand Openings
Etc.

As you can see, there are many instances where you can set up catering services. These are just a few. Almost any event where there's a gather of people can be an opportunity for new business.

Getting Set Up

Once you're determined to offer catering services, you will need to set up some foundations and your pricing structure. When you enter into an agreement with a party, they become a client that requires much more attention than a customer walking up to your truck on the street. You should nurture a relationship with that client and exceed their expectations. It's important not to promise more than what you can deliver. If you do, you are setting yourself up for trouble and a poor experience for you and your client. Sometimes accepting a catering gig means you will miss some of your regularly scheduled street services so you will have to weigh the revenue potential of each event. A signed contract means you are bound to provide the services you promised. So it is important to have a backup plan in case any issues arise like an employee getting ill or mechanical or supply problems.

Menu

If you have an extensive menu, you might want to pare it down and only offer the most popular items for your catering clients. That way you can stock up on only the most used items so you can prepare those dishes on a massive scale. These days you will have to consider the possibilities of offering some special items for those with allergies or even gluten free options. That is not always possible but it is your job to inform your client if you cannot provide those types of options.

Staffing

You will also have to consider the size and pacing of the event you are catering. A large corporate event that lasts several hours may be fast-paced and you will need additional staff to handle the demand. This could be similar to the lunch rush on the streets where the customers are constant until the lunch crowd dissipates. On the other hand, if you are catering a smaller event like a bridal party, the pace at which food needs to be prepared might be a bit slower.

At larger events it might be smart to have someone on-call that can run errands and deliver additional ingredients in case you deplete supplies sooner than expected. You can't easily just shut down at a catering event when you run out of supplies. This will help create a seamless experience for your client and their guests.

Pricing Your Services

Even if you haven't started to offer catering services, you need to consider how much you're going to charge your clients. Are you going to offer packages or ala carte type pricing? This is where a contract is necessary. You may have to consult with a lawyer in order to draw up the contract for your clients to sign. This will protect you and your client in case any issues arise.

Many established caterers offer packages for their clients. By bundling up your services, it makes it easier for your client to decide what they want to buy from you. You also limit the choices for the client and you get to steer them in the direction that makes the most sense for your business. Attractive packages are those that offer a variety of price levels and services so the client know exactly what to expect. Of course there can be deviations to the package so you will have to adjust your prices accordingly or charge an add-on fee. You can even list add-on items so that the client can see that you can accommodate their requests.

To help with pricing, call around and get prices from other caterers and food trucks. Usually you will be discounting your regular prices a bit because the client is purchasing in bulk from you. But you also need to consider your time, staffing costs and any other expenses incurred when determining your prices.

What to Include In a Contract?

If you've never worked with contracts before, it would be a good idea (if possible) to get a hold of some contracts from your competitors and consult with your lawyer. The information in this section should not be taken as actual legal advice but rather just suggestions on what to consider when drawing up a catering contract.

Deposit Amount

One of the first things you need to come up with is the deposit amount you will require from your client to hold a date for them. The deposit tells you that your client is serious about hiring your company for services and it has the ability to keep them bound to their commitment to you. The deposit can be made refundable up to a certain date but you have the option to make it non-refundable if they cancel too close to the event date. Last minute cancellations can cost you money by missing out on other paid events and even costs of supplies needed for the event if you've already started purchasing some.

It's possible that you can hold a date for your client without a deposit but you should limit the time you will keep that hold for them. You don't want to miss out on other opportunities or leads that are more solid.

Liability

This is definitely a conversation for your lawyer but you need to include in writing who is responsible for damages or other unforeseen accidents. Accidents can and will happen eventually so you need to make sure you are covered for this. Your business insurance can help pay for damages but you don't want to have to pay for something you are not ultimately responsible for.

When you provide services at a venue, most places will require that you own some kind of liability insurance. This proof comes typically in the form of a Certificate of Insurance before you are allowed on the premises. There should also be policies on who is responsible for clean-up after event so there are no surprises between any parties involved.

You should also state clearly what happens if you are not able to show up to a scheduled event where all deposits have been paid and guests have been booked. However, everything in your power should be done to fulfill your commitment to your client. If you do not show up for even one event, your reputation could be permanently damaged. Well planned backup plans need to be in place for the most extreme situations.

Marketing Your Catering Service

Long before you launch the catering side of your food truck business, you will have to come up with a plan to promote your additional services. A lot of the marketing strategies and materials will be completely different than how you announce your daily locations throughout the city.

Networking is a key activity for any entrepreneur and you need to build connections in the community so that other businesses and individuals are aware of what you have to offer. Meet with chamber of commerce members and attend their meetings. Feel free to introduce yourself to others and proudly explain what you can do for them and the community.

You should also call and visit the different venues around town that can host events and explain how your food truck would be a great partner with them. This can include hotels, convention centers, churches, festival groups and even event organizers. If you can get on a preferred vendor list, these venues can help promote your services whenever they talk to their clients.

One strategy is to provide a complimentary sampling of your food to the office staff so they can be amazed at what you create. You don't need to go overboard by providing food to a huge office but a good taste sampling can go a long way with decision makers. If you provide an enjoyable experience, they're sure to remember you next time catering services are required.

Another place you can advertise your catering services is on social media. This way you can use your fans to help spread the word. Every once in a while, send out reminders on Twitter, Facebook, Instagram and other social media services you are signed up with. You might also share pictures from events you've catered so your fans can get a glimpse of your food truck in action at a catered event.

And finally, you will need some printed marketing materials that you can give out to people that visit your truck. You might be surprised how many people inquire about having food trucks cater an event they're planning. Often times, the popularity of your food and brand is enough for people to ask but you really need to be proactive to get the word out.

Providing additional services like catering is not easy work but the payoff can make it worthwhile. You can generate additional revenue during times when business is slow. You can fill in some of the hours when your truck is idle and not serving customers. As long as your truck is parked at your commissary, it is not generating income for you. So maximize your efforts and figure out how to reduce the downtime.

Chapter 10 - Major Pitfalls to Avoid

Many people are jumping into the food truck industry expecting to build a business that they can grow and profit from. It is undoubtedly a very exciting and high-profile type of business. New food truck owners are hitting the streets for the first time every month across the country. While the industry is still growing, it is an unfortunate reality that not every food truck owner is going to make a sustainable living at this. There aren't reliable statistics as to how many food truck businesses fail each year but some experts estimate that that the failure rate is upwards of around 60% during the first 3 years of business. This is about the same rate at which restaurants fail.

Before you start doubting the merits of food truck industry you should be aware of some of the factors surrounding those failures. That way, the warning signs can be recognized earlier and preventative action can be taken. There are a lot of misconceptions or lack of knowledge for those who enter this industry. Many believe that just because they are a good cook means they can successfully run a food truck. While being able to create delicious tasting dishes is an integral part of a successful food truck, owners must realize that it is still a business that needs to be treated as a business. It's not necessarily a business you can invest in and just hire people to run it... at least not in the beginning. It takes a lot of hours and hard work to build up a customer base. A lot of growing pains are realized in the early years. And above all, costs need to be effectively managed.

Outsiders do not realize the amount of unseen work that goes into the daily operation of a food truck. There are many hours of preparation time like sourcing ingredients, location scouting, marketing, cooking, packaging and more. In most cases, food truck owners are involved in every aspect of the daily routine and must be prepared and understand this fact. The time commitment alone is enough for some food truck owners to shut down in the first year. Anything worth building takes time to nurture and refine.

A great practice we can borrow from small to medium size restaurants is to keep your menu at a manageable size. Your truck has limited storage space as well as kitchen space. Too many items on your menu means you need more space to store your raw ingredients. If your truck is theme based, then only offer the most popular dishes for the style of food you are serving. That way you can excel at a few dishes and maintain consistency. If you are cooking too many unique items, orders can get mixed up and cause confusion in the kitchen.

Making customers wait can lead to negative feelings toward your truck. Avoid offering dishes that take too long to prepare. Customers who visit food trucks generally expect relatively fast service especially if they've been standing in a long line. In addition, the more people you can move through your line, the greater the profits. Having an efficient process from taking the customer's order to delivering the plated dish greatly benefits you and the customer.

Unexpected expenses can also kill an otherwise promising food truck operation. The daily costs of staying open can make it appear that money is flying out the door constantly. But when you have to pay for unplanned expenses, things really start to get tight. You're already paying for a commissary, propane, ingredients, serving supplies, staffing and more! But often vehicle maintenance gets overlooked. It is inevitable that your food truck will break down. Whether it is the truck itself or the equipment, any kind of repair is costly. To keep costs down, most food truck owners buy old trucks that are prone to mechanical failure. Some vehicle expenses can be manageable but big break downs like transmission failure can severely put a dent in your revenue.

A lack of understanding new technology can also contribute to the demise of a food truck owner. A mobile food entrepreneur needs to have a firm grasp of how social media like Twitter and Facebook can benefit a business. Social media platforms need to work in tandem with your traditional marketing efforts. Maintaining consistency in your cooking, locations and customer service leads to happy customers that know what to expect each time they visit you.
Building and growing a reliable customer base takes time and constant nurturing. Having poor customer service can also turn new and existing customers away. A single instance of treating a customer poorly can lead to a very damaging review on sites like Yelp and Urbanspoon. Customers who have never even tried your truck may brush you off without even sampling your food.

Like anything in life, you only get one chance to make a first impression so make sure you have the right person interacting with your customers. Understanding where the points of failure can come from will better prepare you for these types of situations. Building a successful food truck is not a get rich quick type of business. Hard work, a sound business plan and proper financial management are the solid foundation for any food truck entrepreneur. While it cannot guarantee success, it will give you an advantage over those that are not as well prepared!

Chapter 11 - Conclusion

There is no way that a book can teach every aspect of the food truck industry but I hope that now you have a better understanding of some of the important considerations when it comes to being a gourmet food truck owner. Every truck is different and the dynamics can change considerably from event to event, from location to location and from day to day. It should be treated like any other business with real expenses and strategic planning.

This is definitely one of those businesses where a lot is learned on the job and actually doing the daily tasks. It helps to have partners and employees experience the achievements and all the behind-the-scenes madness that goes on so that each can work toward the goal of making your food truck a success. Operations can be fast and furious if your truck is popular and you'll have to adjust if you find you're having a hard time keeping up.

And even if running the truck is hectic, you can't let your customers know you're having issues. Providing great customer service is one sure way of creating happy customers and will probably return and buy from you again.

This is an exciting industry to be in and it can be a lot of fun but always keep in mind that a food truck business needs to always operate efficiently to remain profitable. You won't find another group of business owners who are as enthusiastic about their businesses as food truck owners. It's a wonderful community of entrepreneurs that support each other.

And finally, as a food truck owner, you are in a unique class of entrepreneurs that likes to get your hands dirty and really be hands-on in all aspects of the business. It involves cooking skills, technology, mechanical skills, problem solving, marketing, logistics and more! Your day starts early and ends late. Embrace it and make a real impact in your life and your customers!

Did you like this book?

I'd like to say thank you for purchasing my book. My goal is to provide the most complete information about food trucks and the industry. I hope you enjoyed it!

As a favor, I would be grateful if you could take a minute and please leave me a review for this book at the website you purchased it from. Your feedback will help me to continue writing and updating the information about the food truck industry.

Thank you!

Andrew Moorehouse

Blog: FoodTruckBusinessPlan.com

Books Available in the Food Truck Startup Series

THE FOOD TRUCK STARTUP

START YOUR OWN FOOD TRUCK
LEAVE THE CORPORATE WORLD BEHIND!

Andrew Moorehouse

THE FOOD TRUCK MARKETING HANDBOOK

ATTRACT MORE CUSTOMERS
EARN MORE PROFITS!

Andrew Moorehouse

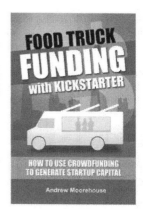

FOOD TRUCK FUNDING with KICKSTARTER

HOW TO USE CROWDFUNDING
TO GENERATE STARTUP CAPITAL

Andrew Moorehouse

FOOD TRUCK BUYER'S GUIDE

BUY, BUILD AND CUSTOMIZE
YOUR OWN FOOD TRUCK

Andrew Moorehouse

FOOD TRUCK MOBILE PAYMENT SYSTEMS

START ACCEPTING MAJOR
CREDIT CARDS LIKE A PRO

Andrew Moorehouse

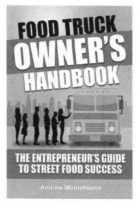

FOOD TRUCK OWNER'S HANDBOOK

THE ENTREPRENEUR'S GUIDE
TO STREET FOOD SUCCESS

Andrew Moorehouse

Made in the USA
Columbia, SC
02 February 2018